This book is dedicated to all the little leaders of the world...

Sondriya books

It did not rain again...

The summer was getting hot and dry.
Every lake and river was dry too.

All the animals got together,
the wise owl,
the great elephant,
the suspicious snake,
the long Giraffe,
the mighty lion,
and even the working ant,
to choose a leader among
them who could see the
farthest.

"We could follow the leader to a new lake", said Mr. Owl.

The lion said...

"I am fast, I should lead us."

The elephant said,

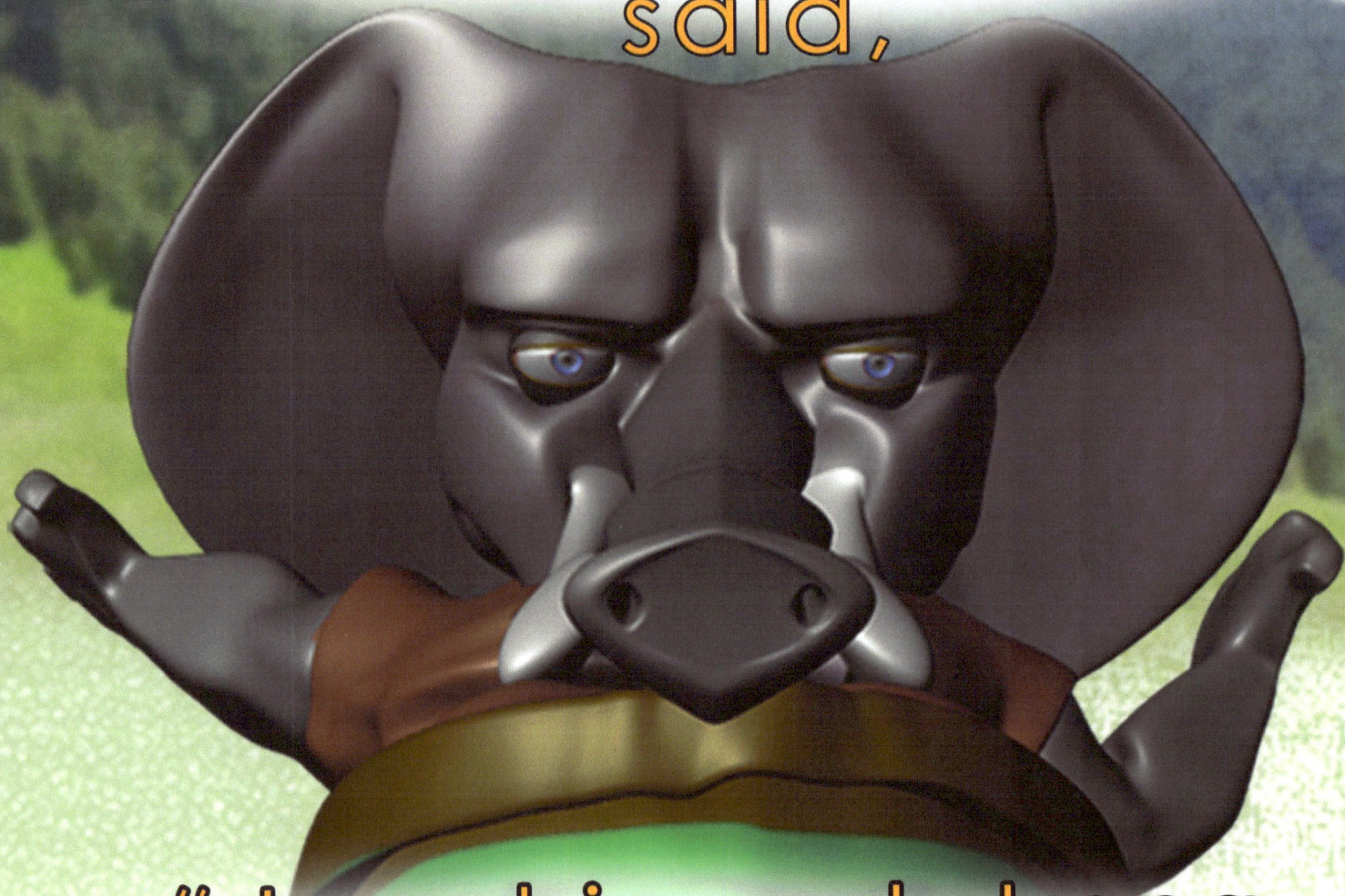

" I am big and strong and I can see very far, I should lead".

The suspicious snake
said,

"I can slide up your back
and onto your trunk to see
even farther, I should be the
leader.

The giraffe said,

"I am taller than both of you put together and could see the furthest, I should be the leader. "

Mr. Owl, although he could fly, he could not see far away.

Everyone argued and fought over who would be the leader.

When a small tiny voice,
near everyone's feet, was
heard saying. . .

"I should be the leader!
I should be the leader!"

Everyone started laughing. The ant looked so tiny, how could she be the leader?

The mighty lion said, "but you are not the strongest."

The great elephant said, "but you are not the biggest."

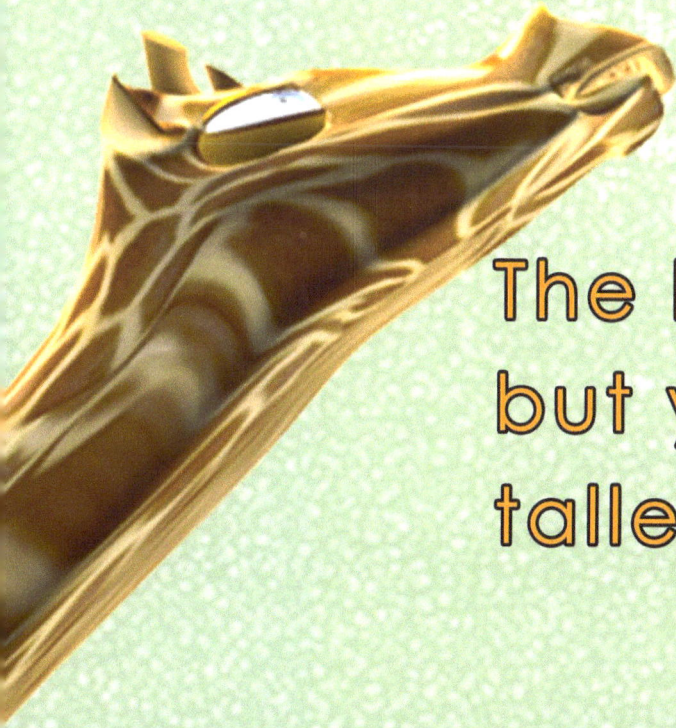

The long giraffe said," but you are not the tallest."

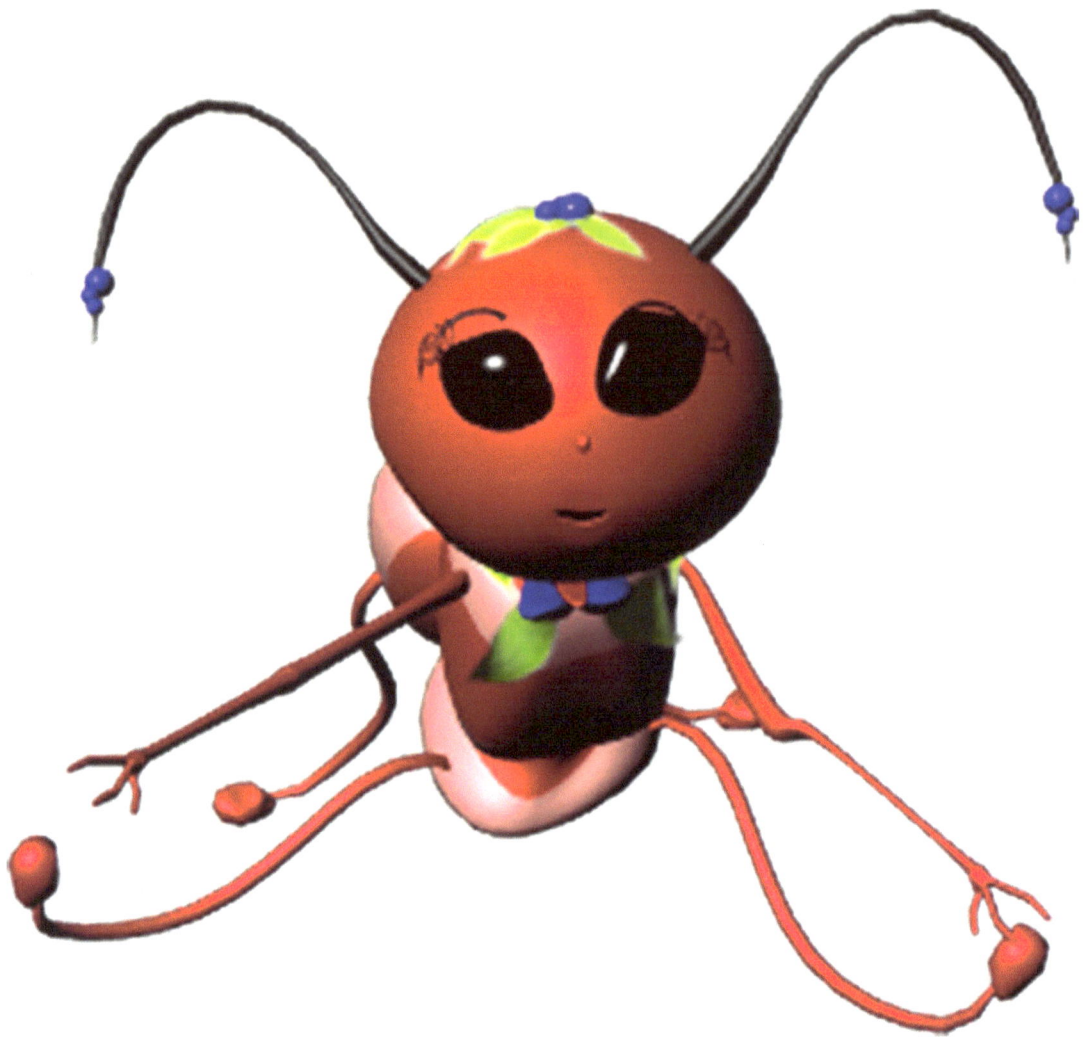

The ant looked up, smiled and said,
" I am not big and I am not tall, but
I can see the farthest of them all.

This puzzled even the wise owl.
"Show us", said the owl.

The ant started climbing up the strongest, largest , and tallest tree.

When she reached the tip top of the tree, all the way to the tip of the top most branch she said...

"Now I am the tallest of all , on the strongest tree, and I can now see a lake far ahead of me. Far to the north is the water we need, follow me so now I can lead."

The animals now instead of laughing at the ant , were thanking the ant. The ant got a ride on the tree and over the elephant's back as the littlest leader led the animals to the new lake.

THE END

Sometimes it takes the littlest to do the biggest...

Sondriya
books

Sondriya books

www.ingramcontent.com/pod-product-compliance
Lightning Source LLC
Chambersburg PA
CBHW042112040426

42448CB00002B/245